# Cow in the Road
# Bear in the House

## UNGUARDED
## LITERARY
## MOMENTS

COW IN THE ROAD ~ BEAR IN THE HOUSE

Compiled & designed by: Roslyn A. Nelson

Little Big Bay LLC

Publisher: Little Big Bay

littlebigbay.com

ISBN 978-0-9892822-1-5

Library of Congress Control Number: 2013908296

# Cow in the Road
# Bear in the House

UNGUARDED LITERARY MOMENTS

Compiled by

Roslyn A. Nelson

DEDICATED

to these three kids
whoever
and wherever they are.

## NOVEMBER 2003

Report of three kids
lying on the hood
of their car
with no lights on
on Highway 2.

Update: They
were looking at
the Northern Lights.

# THANK YOU

Thanks to reporters, editors
and police departments
for recording the good,
the bad and the funny,
year after year.

Thanks to the Wisconsin
Historical Society for preserving
these records and to the archive
services at the Northern Great
Lakes Visitor Center for so kindly
helping me with my research.

# INTRODUCTION

This book is VERY local.

You will "get it" for sure if you live in Northern Wisconsin. However, anyone who has spent time in small American towns will find themselves in familiar territory on these pages.

The anecdotes are from newspapers, primarily police reports from Ashland and Bayfield Counties in Wisconsin. Newspapers that have posted police reports or recorded news of that nature over the years are: the Ashland Daily News, Ashland Daily Press, and Bayfield County Press.

When someone calls the police, they can be angry, worried, fearful or curious but whatever the feelings are, they are always telling a truth about themselves and an event they are focused on. These calls do not begin with "Once upon a time ..."

They start in the middle of the story,
at its dramatic height, and the resulting
unguarded, literary moments allow us
a look into our communal psyche.

In the beginning, I was a frequent visitor,
then I took a leap of faith, bought a small
house and left the big city for good.

It's a common story. Some will tell it for the
first time this year, usually those looking
for a simpler, more rural life. Others (often
musicians, artists, or farmers) remember
arriving here 30 or more years ago.

I wonder if the glimpses of life in this
book might appeal to "immigrants" from
bigger cities more keenly than those who
have lived here all their lives and take
"cows in the road, bears in the house" for
granted. That said, I have laughed over
the police reports with both longtime and
new residents alike, usually prefaced with,
"Listen to this one!"

I have to confess that the laughs do not
outnumber the sad and disturbing calls
that come into the police. But the funny and
endearing calls tell us something wonderful
about ourselves and we can celebrate that.

Callers to the police have unbounded
confidence in law enforcement's ability
to fix things: a duck stuck in a fence,
online scams from Nigeria, or spiders
in the house. It is clear that police in
this part of the world are not the enemy.
Indeed, if someone tried to "Occupy
Ashland," the police might just buy
the coffee.

You will notice, on these pages, that the
police often respond like irritated, wise
parents and simply tell someone to "cut it
out" or "mellow out." No arrest required,
very straightforward.

Prior to the late 1990s, there were no
official police reports in local newspapers
but I've included some fragments which
caught my eye that have the "police report
sensibility." Each one of them offers
a brief flash of bygone times: funny,
tender, amazing, and always revealing.
From a 1923 advertisement: "The Maytag,
all-aluminum, electric washer will make
life worth living, though married."

Midst bar fights and family squabbles
are snippets that show a lighter side and
sometimes, a true innocence or kindness.
Here's an example. 1998: Disabled vehicle
on U.S. Highway 2. Update: Someone went

into town to get them a new fan belt.

It's the ethic around here.

If you see someone you know walking along the road, you might pull over and ask if they need a ride so walking for exercise along a busy road (and there are only two of those) can be complicated.

If you see a car stuck in the snow, you pull over and get out your shovel or jumper cables.

If you get a wrong number, you have a little chat, find out that you live quite near each other and that you've both been seeing a lot of bears lately.

And if your fan belt breaks, don't be surprised if a stranger drives to town to get you a replacement.

Good samaritans aside, mainly people love the police reports because out of the blur of petty crime and domestic disturbance, we discover wry wit, evidence that a simpler time still exists here and there, and an inimitable brand of small-town humor – northern style.

My all-time favorite was a woman who called police to report finding bull semen in her freezer. This succinct police report flooded my brain with questions.

How did it get there? Did this happen very often? And, how did she know what it was?

Friends confidently assured me that it would have been labeled. How do they know? If someone puts bull semen in your freezer as a joke or as an act of revenge, would they label it? Reports like these become honored features on the refrigerator door.

Police reports have no "first chapter" and no conclusion. We never know what came before or how the story ends.

Here's one of my favorites, from 1990. "Request to remove intoxicated male from home. Update: Subject removed, at which point caller invited subject back in to spend the night."

Ah, shucks. "The course of true love never did run smooth."

This book is easy to like. Buy three copies: one for yourself, one for the guest room and one for the outhouse.

– Ros Nelson

# 1883

## DECEMBER 1883

A telephone doctor, said to be expert, held forth in town this week. The hello institution ought to be greatly improved when he gets done with it.

# 1887

## SEPTEMBER 1887

Mollier Bates, drunk and noisy. $10 costs. Sentence suspended upon condition that he would leave the city.

A piece of rock was thrown 2000 feet by a blast in shaft No. 9, Calumet and Hecla Mine, in Michigan, and in coming down, crashed through a house, landing at the feet of an old woman who sat knitting.

Mrs. Ole Mikkelson, a Swedish woman, was bending over, working in the garden when a yearling calf playfully raised on its hind legs and threw its fore feet over her shoulders. The woman started for the house but before she reached the door, she fell to the ground insensible and soon died, it is thought from fright.

## OCTOBER 1887

(Swoon)

Miss Lottie Hanscomb, while horseback riding on 2nd Street, had a very narrow escape from serious injury. Her horse became unmanageable and ran west until caught by Frank Matthews. When the animal was stopped, Miss Hanscomb fell to the ground but was caught by Mr. Matthews.

A Milwaukee woman is suing another for $100, due she alleges, for securing a husband for the defendant.

Mrs. Palmer, a Broadhead widow,
has sued Farmer Curtz for
$10,000 for breach of promise
and Curtz is "all tore up."

A Fort Howard alderman
is charged with setting fire
to a citizen's woodshed to see what
time the fire department would
make in responding to the alarm.

# 1923

## FEBRUARY 1923

Lost – one long, black, silk tassel.
Telephone 40J.

AD: Good Morning Madam.
Washing Day is a Hard Day!
You can turn it into a "Joy Day."
The Maytag, all-aluminum, electric
washer will make life worth living,
though married.

## MARCH 1923

The party who took the clothes
from the line at 607 10th Avenue
is known. Kindly return and no
further proceedings will be taken.

...returning from Washburn,
a Chevrolet having a gay old time
in front of us for quite a while
before we dared to shoot by,
and looking back, we saw three
couples, all Ashlanders in the most
endearing positions imaginable.
If the mothers of those girls could
have seen them ... there would
surely have been some smacking
done, or we are mistaken.
The driver of that car didn't even
have his hands on the wheel.
They were buried somewhere
under ... (dramatic pause) the rim
of the girls' bonnet.

We note that the Ashland banks
have not paid their taxes yet, and
we are in good company.
Neither has the editor.

Glidden was startled yesterday, out of a fine winter's nap, when at about 3:00 in the afternoon, a buck deer blew into town and casually jogged down the main street. ...the City Marshall walked up to the animal and pinched it for speeding. "The traffic and speed laws of Glidden must be observed," said Marshall Eneulinger. The deer is now in the possession of Mr. Stratz who has it in his barn.

Captain Mrs. Nichols left for Washburn where she will spend the day gathering subscriptions for the Self Denial Campaign.

# 1933

## DECEMBER 1933

Chester Olson and young Roland Roy were coasting down Catholic Hill by the Merten's home when the two sleds collided with enough force to knock Roland unconscious.

It is hoped that the children
of Bayfield will confine sledding
to Cooper Hill.

# 1934

## JANUARY 1934

Black, waterproof carriage
robe, good condition.
Will trade for potatoes.

A Model T Ford, owned by Reuben
Bissell of La Pointe, crashed
through the ice on Monday, about
a mile out from La Pointe.

# 1935

## OCTOBER 1935

It will be a sorry day for those
who covered the fronts of several
buildings with lime on Hallowe'en
night, if they are caught.

In the space that an advertisement
might have occupied:
"This space was reserved by
a local merchant who promised
to advertise this week but
FAILED TO KEEP HIS PROMISE."

# 1990

## JANUARY 1990

Report of person sleeping
in front of fireplace at resort
and refusing to move.

Report of mailbox damage
by bowling ball which is
in snow by box.

(if it isn't one thing ...)
1:01 p.m. Report of woman being
harassed by female known to her.
6:02 p.m. Report of woman being
harassed by male—and later,
female—known to her.
7:00 p.m. Report of woman being
harassed by phone.

Report of fight in front of tavern.
Update: Fight was only a couple of
intoxicated people messing around.

Report of theft of three cans
of aerosol whipping cream
from supermarket.

Report of cell phone found
in back of squad car.

Report of marijuana pipe found
in wife's dresser.

Caller reports hearing voices
in her front hallway. Update:
No one in hallway as there
is no front hallway.

Report of two boys fighting
over making toast.

Report of dog devouring
another dog in 500 block
of Chapple Avenue.

Report of bedspread taken
from motel room

(Well, as long as you're
calling a friend ...)
Report of harassing and vulgar
phone calls. Update: Party making
calls was calling friends and
screwing around on the phone but
dialed the wrong number.

Request to remove intoxicated
male from home. Update: Subject
removed, at which point caller
invited subject back in
to spend the night.

# 1997

## JANUARY 1997

Caller requesting assistance
because her back door
was covered with icicles ...

Caller complained that snowmobiles racing around an empty lot were keeping children awake. Update: Snowmobiles were being used to tramp down trail to recreational corridor. Operators promised not to run in circles in the future.

Complaint from man who said his wife came home and went crazy.

Report of open door at business. Employee found inside.

Police received several 911 hang-up calls. The call was traced and officers dispatched to residence. They were advised that there was a sleepover with small children. The mother was advised.

Received report of ice chunk in the road. Officer removed chunk.

# MARCH 1997

Reports of several kids running
across the roof of an apartment
building complex. Officer reports
it looks like kids were sliding
off the roof. Kids he spoke
to denied it but footprints led
directly to the apartment.

Citizen report of two suspicious
people in auto lot. Turned out to be
a couple shopping for a car ...

Sunday ... Two foot ice mound
building up at intersection.
May be a water leak. Water
Department advised to call back
if it gets worse, otherwise they'd
like to wait until Monday.

Report of juveniles climbing
pine tree before bus arrives
each morning.

Stolen sweater complaint.

Received report that someone was trying to enter home without permission.Update: Subject taken to his own home.

Received call stating the paperboy was on the roof of the house.

Ashland's new winter parking regulations are in effect. Today is an odd day.

Man called from Memorial Medical Center asking police to look for his wife who left the hospital with $700 her husband asked her to hold while he was in surgery. Wife was eventually found at a casino.

Dog and cat call from resident who reported cats were pooping under her porch.

# APRIL 1997

(Small town solution: "Don't do it.")
Officers were called to local hotel because guests complained that someone was knocking on their windows. Police found suspect and warned him not to knock again.

Received report that dog was harassing pet rabbits.

Caller reported that portion of Lake Park Road has sunk two and one half feet.

Caller said that while she was partying in Ashland, her car was taken somewhere at sometime by someone. Caller was not sure where she was while making the call.

Request for an officer to the Pig Iron Dock. Caller advised that a big party occurred there and a big mess was left.

Caller reported black ice-fishing
teepee that is still out on the ice
beyond the Coal Dock. Ashland
Fire Department reported ice
conditions were unsafe and
for that reason, would not
inspect the teepee at this time.

## MAY 1997

Report of juveniles riding bikes
in drainage pipes.

Received report of three young
girls doing their homework
in the street.

Memorial Medical Center employee
reported a bear hanging around
the treatment center.

Received report from Ashland
County Sheriff's Department that
a duck has its head stuck
in a fence. Officers dispatched
and duck freed.

Received complaint that when an employee went to take out the garbage, a person jumped out of the dumpster.

(No more Mr. Nice Guy)
Call from area supermarket to report they've had an individual shoplift seafood from their store several times and they'd like to see an officer.

Received call that two young kids were still outside their home. Complainant said they told him that their mother wouldn't let them in. Police reported mother said she didn't want them in because she had just cleaned the floors and they weren't dry yet. Kids reported playing catch and had no problem with being in the yard.

## JUNE 1997

A truck with a load of ball bearings spilled about 100 ball bearings on MacArthur Avenue.

Received report that three city benches were in the 400 block of Main Street when there should be only one.

## JULY 1997

(Highly motivated)
Person attempting to enter the Memorial Medical Center mental health wing through locked door.

Caller reported that someone had dropped four kittens on her porch. Officer advised caller that he would call dog warden.

Officers took a call from a female complainant who said she could hear people wrestling in the bushes near her home.

(In July?)

Officers advised to be on the lookout for anyone trying to ride a snowmobile around town.

Lost wallet found in 200 block of 3rd Street West. Wallet apparently had been missing for decades. Returned to owner.

Caller very upset about lost puppy. As dispatcher takes information, puppy begins to scratch at back door. Caller very excited. Dispatcher excited too.

## OCTOBER 1997

Received report of a person hit by a fawn.

Report of a dog attempting to enter rabbit pen.

Fire alarm from area church. False alarm set off by burning food.

*(Floated away?)*
Received report that parade float was in the 400 block of 11th Avenue. Float returned to yard.

Ashland County Sheriff's Department received a call that people were making pot brownies.

*(Where DOES a dummy belong?)*
Vandalism call. Dummy lying in middle of street. Officer located dummy and placed it back where it belonged.

## DECEMBER 1997

Report of students drinking wine and whiskey at hockey game at Northland College and possibly threatening players from Hibbing. Person selling tickets says it's usually like this at the games.

Restaurant worker advised that a customer had a parrot in the restaurant and refused to leave.

Officers dispatched. Parrot and
owner left building.

# 1998

## JANUARY 1998

Thursday 9:40 p.m. Two cars
sprayed with chocolate syrup.
Friday 8:39 a.m. Laundry
soap and chocolate syrup
sprayed on van.

Woman on way to work reported
maroon truck stopped, man naked
except for shoes exited vehicle
and urinated on highway.

Man said woman's car is stuck
in his driveway and he has
to get to work. Called back and
said woman had returned with
someone in another vehicle to pull
her out. Called again to report
both cars stuck.

(1,000 clowns?)

4:20 a.m. Burglary, breaking and entering report. Woman woken by man in bedroom. Another man was also in house. Both left, followed by woman's husband.

(And if you believe that ...)

Caller said he saw two juvenile males purchasing eggs for what he believed was throwing at people and/or vehicles. Caller said she overheard them say, "Look at these bombs" and "These would be great." Officer investigated and reports teenagers were on their way home to make scrambled eggs.

## FEBRUARY 1998

Report of stud horse in corral with registered mare due to be bred in April. Stud may have gotten to mare.

Abandoned bicycle on roof at church next to Bay Theater.

(Offer him tea?)
Report of strange dog sitting on
porch. People afraid dog is mean.


Hitchhiker who had passed out in
car was dropped off at Memorial
Medical Center. Update: Hitchhiker
only wanted a ride home.


6:33 p.m. Two children
at Civic Center not picked
up by their mother.
7:12 p.m. Children in custody.
7:30 p.m. Mother called to report
two missing children.


Verbal disturbance reported.
Investigation revealed man was
angry over a haircut he had just
received and didn't like.


Female reported that kids were
coming into her basement all the
time with big shipments of drugs
and also have been coming through
a hole in her roof.

Car entered and nothing taken but caller would like bear trap set in yard to catch people.

## MARCH 1998

Report of manure dumping in ditch beside road. Perpetrator said he pays county taxes and he can do anything he wants.

## APRIL 1998

Iron River resident received a scam letter from Nigeria.

Report of three kids sitting in house when owner came home. Owner knew two of them. Kids said they were just listening to music. Nothing missing except some food.

## MAY 1998

Report of boys not wanting to go to school.

Report of a carload of intoxicated
women heading west on U.S. 2.

Report of police tape around
building containing couple who
were married previous night.
Wanted to know if tape was being
used as "do not disturb" sign.

Resident called to inform that they
would be cutting a tree down
and it would land in the street.

Mother reported her son dazed
after drinking some water.

Husband requests documentation
that wife is not home.

Caller wants assistance getting his
clothes back from his wife.

Report of black widow spider
found in home and flushed
down the toilet.

Report of theft of trees and
rhubarb from private property.


## JUNE 1998

Report of disabled vehicle
on U.S. Highway 2.
Update: Someone went into town
to get them a new fan belt.


Bear reported in line of traffic
on Highway 63.


Report of large bear walking south
on 10th Avenue West.


Woman says people in attic are
still selling drugs and stealing
water and cups. No entrance
to attic found in house. Woman
assured that officers would patrol
and shine lights on attic regularly.


Suspicious activity reported. Wire
cut on snow fence and boxes of
frosting put in cupboard.

Man threatened by woman known to him who called and said, "You'd better watch your f&%$#@ back."

Report of dog chasing people and ruining clothing in Iron River.

Report of person going through their mail on Mattson Road.

Report of men living in basement stinking up the place and stealing canning lids.

7:37 a.m. Caller reported a man reading her newspaper in her home. Man seemed familiar ...

Horse and bull out for a stroll on County A.

Report of door ajar in house. Owner reported it was left that way so cats would come and go.

## JULY 1998

Report of a nine-year-old boy
bitten by a chipmunk.

Report of male walking down Main
Street breaking trees and tossing
them into roadway.
Suspect en route to jail.

Report of someone sneaking
around daughter's house. Update:
Person outside was daughter.

Car reported stolen, later found.
Keys left on porch with note that
said, "I'm sorry."

Report of outhouse being pushed
into bathing beach.

## AUGUST 1998

Reckless driving report. Older
couple came within three feet of
woman walking on Big Bay Road.

Report of man entering convenience store, drinking three bottles of NyQuil and walking out. Update: Person apprehended and taken for treatment. Officer at gas station to find out cost of NyQuil.

Report of a large piece of plywood about to fall off roof of City Hall. Plywood that keeps pigeons out of the attic had become loose.

Male in sleeping bag found on Highway 2.

Report of car/deer accident. Request to keep deer carcass.

(No rush ...)
Report of dead cat in front of house. Informed that cat would be removed after lunch.

Ambulance request for man who ran over himself with his own car. Ambulance not wanted by victim.

# SEPTEMBER 1998

Report of being passed on the
right on Main Street by
a turquoise vehicle.

Boyfriend pinched woman
with jumper cables.

New owner walking his land found
marijuana plants growing there.
Update: Plants pulled up.

Report of 25 phone calls recorded
on caller ID made to woman from
someone named Joe.

Report of large number of youths
not in school. Update: Drinking
party at Morgan Falls.

Report of trees on County Road
off County C blocking traffic.
Person said they were given
permission to block road.

Older couple reported they had lost
$500 which the man was carrying
in a small wallet in his sock.

## OCTOBER 1998

Report of trailer broken into
by person who slept in bed
and drank owner's pop.

Caller worried because she took
Excedrin instead of Tylenol.

Report of man in lawn chair sitting
in middle of Sanborn Avenue.
Update: Man is race official.

Noise complaint from Fifield Row.
Sailboat sails are flapping
against poles.

Ferret answering to name
of Fivel Lynn is missing.

Rock taken from yard.

Caller reported three strangers
in his home. Update: Men were
friends of his daughters but father
was screaming at them
"as he usually did."

Car sprayed with shaving cream.

Report of man sitting on white line
in highway north of Marengo.

A live, red fox was reported
touring the 10th Avenue West
neighborhood.

## NOVEMBER 1998

(Whoops ...)
Man returned home and found his
belongings in the dumpster. He
said that neighbors in downstairs
apartment were to have been
evicted and landlord may have
gotten their apartment mixed up
with his apartment.

Half loaf of banana bread
stolen from kitchen.


Theft of knobs off porch
on St. Claire Street.


Caller concerned over knock on
door with no one there.
Update: Daughter-in-law at door.


## DECEMBER 1998

Report of person dumping bags
of garbage full of adult diapers on
highway in town of White River.


(Well, that sucks ...)
Man who said he was a vacuum
cleaner salesman but having no ID
attempted to gain entrance
to home in Village of Butternut.


Disorderly conduct report. Person
in tavern causing problems.
Update: Girlfriend showed up and
dragged him out of the bar.

(Been in there lately, Mom?)
Report of marijuana growing
operation found in son's room.

Report of house fire. Two foot
flames in kitchen with person "just
sitting there." Update: Subject
was lighting hand warmers which
caused a huge flame which is what
person who reported fire saw.

Report of person walking around
house leaving tracks in snow.

Report of neighbors letting their
dogs loose and "looking for
someone to sue."

Report of people banging
on door and raising hell.

Many calls reporting an
unidentified flying sled at various
locations in Ashland.
Update: Further investigation
revealed it was Santa Claus.

Report of door blowing
open on house.

Report of cows being neglected
Update: Livestock were beef cattle,
not cows. They had a pole bar for
shelter but chose to remain outside.

# 1999

## JANUARY 1999

Report of car on fire.
Update: Someone smoking
in the back seat.

Report of kids improperly dressed
for the weather.

Report of overly friendly elk
on Bibon Road.

*(She kept an eye on him ...)*
Woman at ice rink saw man
urinate on snowbank. A short time
later he repeated the offense.

Monday, 7:37 a.m. Car in ditch.
7:55 a.m. Another car in ditch.
8:18 a.m. Car in ditch.
9:10 a.m. Car in ditch.
10:25 a.m. Snowmobile went into
Lake Namekagon.
11:58 a.m. Car in ditch.
1:44 p.m. Car in ditch due to
driver falling asleep.
3:55 p.m. Car in ditch.
5:23 p.m. Car in ditch.
7:09 p.m. Car on fire.

(Collars on sale?)
Report of German Shepherd
trying to get into hardware store.

## FEBRUARY 1999

Report of attempted house
break-in. Shortly before that,
woman received phone call from
a male asking her to open the
door. Update: It was woman's
mother who had forgotten her key.

Report of muskrat loose in
basement of courthouse. Update:
Critter caught in garbage can and
awaiting animal control officer.

(Friend or terrorist?)
Report of large, friendly dog
hanging around playground and
terrorizing children.

Report of woman receiving
seven harassing phone calls
by person known to her.
Update: Caller warned to
knock it off.

Vandalism report: Individuals
shooting paint balls at house.
Update: Neighbor boy was shooting
at his garage and missed.
Was to apologize to neighbor and
learn how to aim better.

(Bear or decorator?)
Report of screen door of house
ripped, tracks all over home and
things changed inside residence.

(Shapeshifter)

Report of someone hiding
behind Stuntz Bridge. Update:
Appears to be someone hiding but
was actually part of the bridge.

## MARCH 1999

Report of smoldering bar stool
at a business in the Village of
Butternut. Update: Damage
appeared to be accidental.

## APRIL 1999

Report of man known to
complainant giving keys to
her house to woman, who has
destroyed bras and stolen five
bags of cookies.

Woman heard from eight-year-old
girl that female known to woman
had put sugar in her gas tank.
Update: the gas was tasted
by officer who advised there
was no sweet taste.

## JUNE 1999

Report of missing woman last
seen at Memorial Medical Center.
Update: Woman was found asleep
in the emergency room.

Report of two women causing
a disturbance. Update: Women
were exchanging children.

Report of 25 Holsteins
on County C. Update: All rounded
up and back in field.

## OCTOBER 1999

10:57 Report of cream of corn
being poured over vehicle with can
placed on top of car. Next day,
10:21 a.m. Male calling to tell that
his mother's vehicle was
also corned.

Report of 25-30 cows on private
property chewing on house.

Loud party complaint. Warning
issued but subject said he would
continue his activities as he did not
particularly like police officers.

Report of grape jelly thrown
at door of house.

Report of suspicious salesperson
trying to demonstrate a product.

(Police watching the watcher?)
Report of man known to
complainant watching her through
garage window. Update: Man was
standing outside garage window
and watching woman's
every move.

Female caller reports while
she was at local grocery store,
a known serial killer has
approached her and asked to stay
at her house overnight.

# NOVEMBER 1999

Request to pick up raccoon.


Report of vehicle heading into
Washburn with buck in the back.


Report of noise pollution.


1:20 a.m. Report of waitress at
strip show bar being grabbed on
the butt. When asked if she wanted
to file a complaint she said she
guessed so but repeated that she
did not know the names of the
persons who grabbed her.


Report of son under house arrest
not at home.
Update: Son located in closet ..


# DECEMBER 1999

(Mondays are like that.)
Monday, 6:35 p.m.
Report of male going nuts.

Report of woman known to victim
calling his relatives and telling
them he was dead.

(Thief invisible from waist down.)
Report of theft of camouflage pants
from clothesline.

Report of head being taken
from 3-D deer target.

Report of cow in road.

# 2000

## MARCH 2000

Report of clothes oiled on
clothesline on Birch Hill.

4:59 p.m.
Report of vehicle through ice
off Roy's Point Marina.
5:55 p.m.
Report of large hole in ice.

Report of wounded pigeon
outside motel.


(Ice canoeing?)
Report of black lab falling though
ice on Lake Namekagon. Update:
Dog rescued by man in canoe.


## APRIL 2000

Caller reports a small, gray vehicle
with three people on top of it.


## MAY 2000

Report of vandalism to billboard.
"See your local Dodge dealer"
was changed to "See your local
Drug dealer."


Report of cat hiding under porch
and eating birds at bird feeder.

# JULY 2000

Report of driver in van giving the "finger" to woman.

Report of a cigarette that has started a dish cloth on fire underneath the kitchen sink.

Thursday 3:21 a.m. Report of bear running through bank parking lot. 8:46 a.m. Bear sighted in ravine near 11th Street. Noon - Report of bear in 2000 block of W. 6th Street. Saturday 2:04 p.m. Report of bear in dumpster at 315 Turner Road. 11:50 p.m. Report of bear in tree at 600 block of 12th Avenue West.

Report of snow cone from vendor on Main Street being contaminated with rat poison. Update: Customer and cone returned to vendor who ate the cone with no ill effects.

Report of "thing that turns on water outside" missing.

Report of man laying in the street
at 1200 W. Main Street. Update:
Man was waiting for a ride.

Report of ceramic dwarf lawn
ornament in 200 block
of 14th Avenue East.

9:22 p.m. Received complaint
from irate citizen that frogs were
keeping him awake.

(Better to use boat in water)
Report of sailboat mast damaging
power line in front of Maggies
in Bayfield.

## SEPTEMBER 2000

Report of irate male requesting
lights at ball park be shut off
"before he shoots them out."
Update: Subject was reminded that
it was only 10:30 and recently
it was daylight at that hour.
Subject swore and hung up phone.

Report of an intoxicated male
setting up lawn chair on highway
near Odanah and refusing to move.

(What happened to Male A?)
10:02 p.m. Report of wrestling
match between two males over
giving a woman a ride home.
Update: Woman had left with Male
B before officers arrived. 10:29
p.m. Request from woman to have
Male B removed from her home.

## NOVEMBER 2000

Report of boat in road.

(Lunch rush?)
11:41 p.m. Report of young adults
in parking lot running from car
to car. Update: Only employee
vehicles found in parking lot.

Report of what looks like an elk
brought in by people insisting
it is a big doe.

Woman reports a break-in to her residence. Says all she notices missing is some cologne.

Report of white object floating in Lake Superior.

## DECEMBER 2000

Caller states she cannot see to drive.

Report of sauna on fire.

# 2001

## JANUARY 2001

Home burglar alarm set off. Flying squirrels responsible for alarm.

Report of a cub bear residing in a travel trailer. Update: Department of Natural Resources saw the bear roaming around and saw no need for action.

# FEBRUARY 2001

Report of kids throwing snowballs.

Report of squirrel trapped
in basement.

Report of snowball fight
with snowballs hitting home
instead of kids.

Report of truck going through
the ice near where the ice
road would be.

Report of vehicle attempting
to cross ice road with front
tires through ice.

# MARCH 2001

Report of accident.
UPS truck vs. fire hydrant.

Report of stolen shoes off porch.
Update: Shoes returned.

# APRIL 2001

Report of problem with bear
on porch of house.
Owner feeds his pets outside.
(And now he has a new one.)

Report of two people and tents
on floating ice in Raspberry Bay.
Update: Subjects contacted and
said they would continue
fishing until 5:00 p.m.

# MAY 2001

Report of eight deer in yard,
causing a nuisance. Wants report
made to the Department
of Natural Resources.

Report of couple being attacked
by demons. Couple was using Ouija
board that told them they would
be attacked by demons.

Report of kids on roof of tavern
with beer in their hands.

Report of call asking for the
"weed man" and asking how
much a gram was.

Report of bear trying
to enter house.

Report of two males on roof
of theater smoking dope
in their underwear.

Loud music complaint regarding
Bohemian Hall. Update: Wedding
will be over in 15 minutes.

Report of people cleaning fish at
flowing well on private property.

Report of person in vehicle in
driveway of home blowing horn.
Update: Person blowing horn was
waiting for complainant.
Both were told to mellow out.

# JUNE 2001

Theft of sausage at market.

Oil lamp shades stolen from home.

Report of an intoxicated male
sitting on roadside. Update: It was
a college student observing nature,
watching a deer.

Report of fawn hanging
around area.

Report of black bear cub swimming
at Ashland Marina.

Raccoon stumbling and
not afraid of people.

Report of bear sniffing outside
bedroom window. Subject told to
turn on lights and make noise.

Report of a plastic, cow lawn
ornament stolen.

# JULY 2001

Report of a vehicle parked on the
side of the street with an older
man hunched over.
Update: Man fine, just looking
for four-leaf-clovers.

Report of a bear frequently
walking through back yard.

Report of man sitting outside social
services without pants.
(Ashland County)

Report of man running around
without pants in Red Cliff area.
(Bayfield County)

Report of rattlesnake in yard.
Update: Only a hog snake.

Report of a stolen sewer line.
Update: Found nearby,
appears bear moved it.

Report of sewage truck
leaking contents.

## AUGUST 2001

Report of kid trying to throw lawn
mower over bridge rail.

Report of customers refusing
to pay their bill and refusing
to leave the restaurant.

Report of female in middle
of highway with lots of luggage,
screaming at passing traffic.

Report of objects hovering in sky.

Report of theft of apples from tree.

Report of 7-year-old boy being hit
by rock thrown by another child.
Update: Children were advised
to ignore each other until they
can be friends.

Report of skunk in front of AmericInn, not letting guests in or out of the motel. Update: animal gone when officers arrived.

## SEPTEMBER 2001

Stray cat terrorizing neighborhood.

Report of 3 separate fights going on at tavern in Sanborn.

10:40 a.m. Report of an intoxicated man with a dead skunk in a bag, refusing to leave store. 12:08 p.m. Report of an intoxicated man with a dead skunk in a bag, refusing to leave tavern.

Report of 4 goats on back porch.

Report of someone raising a fawn.

Request for extra patrol at cemetery due to high traffic flow and partying there.

## OCTOBER 2001

Report of man thinking he is being
stalked by police. Police are in area
to investigate skunk report.


Loud party complaint.
Update: Disturbance was 2 kids
having a pillow fight.
Kids were told to go to bed.


Report of 8-year-old driving
a pickup truck.


Report of neighbor flying over
complainant's house repeatedly.
Update: Neighbor is in Superior,
not flying over house.


Report of 3 males running west in
600 block of Main Street, wearing
hair masks and clear gloves.
Update: Three said they were bored
and were sanitizing the town.

# NOVEMBER 2001

Report of toilet paper
in port-a-potty lit on fire.


Report of a strange man, visually
intoxicated, walking near Ferry
Landing on Madeline Island.
Wearing red jacket with "Doc"
printed on sleeve and wears a red
clown nose to harass people.


Report of six head of beef cattle
in parking lot of church.


Report of three males leaving IGA
with 22 dozen eggs en route
to a residence. Update: Subjects
ran from officer but 17 dozen
eggs were recovered.


Report of bed spread in mail
wrapped in white plastic. Recipient
was afraid to open same.
Update: Object was a bed spread.

Report of kids playing flashlight tag in Bayfield Cemetery.

Report of green and moldy oven mitts in linen room at area hotel. Employee concerned about anthrax. Update: Employer not concerned; moldy oven mitts commonly thrown out.

Report of suspicious bag on road in Iron River. Update: Bag appears to contain rabbit food.

Report of suspicious man wearing handcuffs at an area restaurant.

## DECEMBER 2001

Report of a mink in bait shop.

Woman reports of some cars parked on the street, a cat walking down the sidewalk and Olivia Newton-John on the TV.

Report of a man wandering the
back hallway of grocery store
wearing women's clothing.

Report of computer and mouse
floating near marina.

# 2002

## JANUARY 2002

Report of three snowmobiles on
airport runway.

Report of jumper cables stolen
while truck was at service shop.
Cables were of sentimental value.

Person drove a snowmobile to
private residence and dropped off
a cat during the night.

Report of animal shelter broken
into. Money and kittens missing.

Report of man standing on deck
of house muttering to himself.

Tuesday
8:20 a.m. Report of car in ditch
by Best Western.
9:59 a.m. Report of car in ditch
near Marengo.
10:56 a.m. Report of car in ditch
near Mason.
4:31 p.m. Report of car in ditch
near Deer Creek Road.
4:35 p.m. Report of car in ditch
south of White River Hill.
5:27 p.m. Report of car in ditch
near Daley and Blueberry Roads.
Wednesday
12:02 a.m. Report of car in ditch
on Oak Street, New Odanah.

## FEBRUARY 2002

Report of six sleds dogs pulling
unoccupied sled.


Report of intoxicated male
at resort with arms full of ribs.

Report of auto accident.
Vehicle vs. car wash.

Reports of strange lights
in Benoit area.

Report of girl refusing to get
up and go to school.

Received a complaint from a
Washburn mayoral candidate that
a neighbor was displaying another
mayoral candidate's sign on their
side of the fence.

Report of Mayoral sign
stolen in Washburn.

Report of a woman screaming.
Update: She was only venting.

Report of two males throwing
bowling ball into the air and letting
it crash to the ground.

Man threatened by mother-in-law.

Report of illegal garbage dumping
in dumpsters, possibly with
a shrew in the bag.

## MARCH 2002

Report from discount store truck
driver that the back door of his
semi had opened and boxes of
merchandise were on the road
near Grand View. Update: Officer
found one box of cookies but
cookies were already gone.

Report of loose dog in
supermarket.

Report of sauna on fire.

Report of break-in. Update:
No crime. Doorknob has fallen off.

Report of kids on roof of Dairy
Queen in Washburn throwing
snowballs at vehicles.

Report of a resident on the East
Side keeping a baby goat and
selling five vehicles from his yard.

Truck trapped in a car wash.

## APRIL 2002

Report of couch dropped in middle
of 14th Avenue East. Update:
Couch moved to side of road.
(Looks so much better there...)

Report of four patrons
still sitting in tavern.

Report of three males
sitting in parked car.

Report of group of kids yelling and
screaming. Update: Group was an
aspiring band practicing lyrics.

Complainant reported a bear
on his deck that he does
not want to leave.

Report of shot through satellite
dish. Update: Couldn't confirm as
dish was under water at the time.

Report of child putting
on handcuffs and not being able
to get them off.

## AUGUST 2002

Report of suspicious male
with goatee hanging around
Main Street.

Report of people shining flashlights
into trees. Update: Subjects were
building a shack.

Report of vehicle vs. tree.

Report that a car has struck a
house by the post office... driver of
car thought he had put it in park
and when he got out, the car rolled
into the house. Driver and house
owner to work things out.

Report of a cow running
down the middle of the street
near the casino.

Report of heated argument in
church parking lot.

Report of cows headed toward the
highway from the field.

Report of male walking into man's
field with a tub full of green
plants; not responding to yells.

Report of e-coli found in dumpster.

## SEPTEMBER 2002

Report of theft of picture and clock
from man's home. Update: Man
found the items behind his freezer.
They had fallen off the wall.

Report of skinny wolf trotting
across Highway 2.

Report of crazy woman taking
pictures of man in his yard.

Report of ongoing problem with
bear scratching woman's windows.

## NOVEMBER 2002

Report that a wooden garbage can
and lots of eggs are in the road.

Request for officer for assistance
in getting juvenile female
out of bed.

Report of suspicious activity in
the woods near Bark Bay Road.
Update: Men were cutting boughs.

Report of a threatening male deer
which frequents a residence and
is causing concern for attack.

Report of concern of hunters
mistaking his buffalo for deer.

## DECEMBER 2002

Report of a neighbor running
a hose outside and flooding the
street; said she was making
an ice rink for her kids.

Theft of a 4-foot, lighted wreath
from the Fish Lipps Bar.

# 2003

## FEBRUARY 2003

Report of a woman being harassed
by her pastor.

Report of large pigs
roaming free in roadway.

## APRIL 2003

Caller reported her neighbor came
over and put shampoo in her kettle
and would like a deputy to stop
and smell the tea kettle.

## MAY 2003

Caller reported when he arrived home there was a man in his house drinking wine and opening bottles of wine.
Unknown who the man was.

Report of two ponies walking on Whiting Road towards the highway. Update: Officers located the animals which were miniature donkeys. Owner contacted and arrangements made to round up the wee wanderers.

Report of loud music. Update: At midnight, man played one song on his stereo to celebrate his birthday.

## JUNE 2003

Caller reported a flower planter had been tipped over and she thought someone was purposefully killing her hanging-flowers-in-a-basket.

Caller reported a hole in the road.
The hole is 5 feet wide
and 20 feet deep.

Report of loose cattle on highway.
Update: Cows were rounded up.

Report of three cows loose on
County C next to C-Side Bar.

Caller reported a white horse with
black spots rolling in his newly
planted garden.

Report of suspicious activity with
banging noise from neighbors.
Update: Neighbor was doing
house repairs.

Report of individual sitting
in the middle of Highway 13
near Bayfield.

Caller requested to speak with
animal control regarding problem
with pigeons.

Caller reported there was a fox on his porch that would not go away.

# JULY 2003

Cow wandering on Wannabo Road.

Caller reported individuals running a snowmobile (This is July) across the lake and as a result, it sank. Were in process of retrieving it with a pontoon boat.

Many cows loose on the highway.

Strange horse at residence.

Caller reported seeing a logging truck traveling on Lenawee Road with its boom up, taking out power lines as it went.

Caller reported a break-in through window. Update: Realtor showing house but didn't have keys.

Caller reported that he would be
filming a horror movie for college
and would be using a body bag and
someone dressed up, filming
to take place Thursday
on Fish Creek Bridge.

Caller reported watching two boys
break into a cabin. Update: Were
grandchildren of the owner.

Ashland Ford employee
reported finding kittens
among their vehicles.

Caller, age 9, stated someone
poured milk all over him and
wanted a deputy to come
to the house.
Mother also wanted the deputy.

Herd of cattle on Peacy Road.
Cattle were herded back into
pasture by relatives.

# AUGUST 2003

Caller reported that someone left a vase full of flowers on her steps with a note attached that didn't make any sense.

# SEPTEMBER 2003

Thursday 6:29 p.m. Report of several cows blocking the road.
Friday 8:08 p.m. Report of an emaciated white cow.
Sunday 8:13 p.m. Caller reported all cows gone and she had no way to get them back.

Report of a car/bear accident. Driver allowed to keep bear.

# OCTOBER 2003

Caller reported that her neighbor was burying a mobile home. Wanted to know if it was legal. Update: Not legal. Matter turned over to the DNR.

Caller stated that he found a bone that he thought looked suspicious and not a deer bone.

Caller reported a woman "shooting the moon" in front of the Superbowl in Washburn.

Report of a street sweeper on fire on Manypenny Avenue.

## NOVEMBER 2003

Caller reported someone in field harvesting willow.

Blue jay trapped in dwelling.

Report of theft of onion, tomato, and green pepper by person known to victim.

Report of three kids lying on the hood of their car with no lights on, on Highway 2. Update: They were looking at the Northern Lights.

Caller reported two males causing disturbance by burying his door in snow.

## DECEMBER 2003

Suspicious activity of someone in house near a church near the Four Corners Bar. Officer determined it was the person providing church services for the church this week.

Report of a small, female child chasing after a black lab.

# 2004

## JANUARY 2004

Report of needing assistance in opening an apartment door thought to be frozen. Officer was able to open the door by turning the knob.

# FEBRUARY 2004

Complaint about an Evergreen
Shopper paper carrier throwing
papers carelessly. A paper got
sucked into his snowblower.

Caller requested assistance in
getting a stray cat stuck in the
rafters of pole building. They got
the cat down and decided to keep it.

# MARCH 2004

Report of an assault
by JC Penneys on Main Street.

Caller reported finding a stolen cell
phone in the toilet of a bar. Needed
plumber to retrieve it.

The exterior doors of a school had
been super glued and custodian had
to force his way into school.

Report of a suspicious-looking
male loitering in Washburn,
carrying a guitar case.

Caller saw a large, black bear
walking north on Clair Street
towards ore dock. Officer determined it to be a large, black lab.

## APRIL 2004

Report of a vehicle hitting
a parked car and driver tried
to flee. However, vehicles
were stuck together.

Caller reported three horses
loose and were in his field
harassing her horses.

## MAY 2004

Loud music complaint.
Update: Nine-year-old asked to play
guitar inside home.

Caller reported a cult that had
moved in ...

Caller reported smoke or steam
coming from the shower room
at Memorial Park.

Report of a camper on fire.

## JUNE 2004

Caller reported seeing a large,
flaming object in the sky near
Glidden. Officer thought it was
probably fireworks.

Caller reported being nipped by
large dog in the cemetery. She also
believes that the dog is stealing
flowers from the graves.

Caller reported that her neighbors
chickens are roosting in her yard.

Owner reported a male sunning
himself on a picnic table
at Gruenkes in Bayfield,
refusing to leave.

Report of bear cub in dumpster
with mother bear refusing to leave
area. Update: Cub removed and
animals went on their way.

# JULY 2004

Caller reported a male lying under tractor. Cable Fire Department responded but farmer was just taking a nap.

Caller reported a suspicious male wearing a black trench coat and a patch over one eye, on Range Line Road.

Caller reported a couple of juveniles outside her window giggling, in the Town of Russell.

Report of two naked people on beach.

Caller reported that sometime on Friday she lost her purse somewhere in Bayfield.

Criticom called in with a fire alarm - smoke in the kitchen. False alarm; babysitter burned the pizza.

Report of male lying in ditch.
Update: Subject was resting on his
way to Duluth.

Caller reported that someone
broke the tampon machine
and stole the money.

Caller reported wild cat or raccoon
living in a trailer home
to be moved.

Caller reported that a neighbor's
dog had chased someone and had
them trapped on the porch.

Caller reported that someone
had dropped bag of fish innards
on his mailbox.

Report that a male went into the
ladies' restroom at a local park
and washed dishes.

Report of a deer dropping dead
in person's yard.
Update: Investigation showed that
deer hadn't been shot.

# AUGUST 2004

Caller stated that a skunk with a cup stuck on its head was running around his house on Willis Avenue.

Caller reported the "biggest bear she'd ever seen" in her garage, on Main Street East.

Caller reported a car with "just married" on it driving erratically and almost hitting a parked car.

Caller was concerned about several small children standing on the breakwall catching the spray from the high waves.

Report of deer jumping into trailer and getting wedged under kayaks.

Young couple behaving inappropriately on a lawn in Washburn.

Report that someone had dumped a bunch of lawn mowers on his property on Blue Moon Road.

# SEPTEMBER 2004

Caller reported a vehicle dragging
a mattress behind it with kids
on the mattress.

Caller reported a male in laundry
room at The Lumberman's with
only a towel on. Male was washing
his jeans and had no other
clothing to put on.

Complainant reported someone
had tipped over his outhouse
and glued his doors shut.

Report of about 25 cows walking
down Wannabo Road.

Caller stated that her boyfriend
left about a week ago and wants
to know how long she has to
wait before she can throw all his
belongings out.

Caller stated he has some vagrants
living in his basement and
he wants them removed.

Caller reported that the driver in front of her hit a deer and kept on driving. She put the deer into her trunk and didn't know what to do with it.

Caller reported theft of large pumpkin from his pumpkin patch.

Caller reported her neighbor's ducks and geese were in her trout pond, eating her trout. Neighbor refused to respond.

## OCTOBER 2004

Request for officer intervention for owner to get their dog back. People who had babysat the dog for two weeks now want to keep the dog.

Horse heading east on Highway 2.

Caller reported that someone tied a rope across County Road E.

Landlord refused to get rid of fleas in an apartment.

Report of hunters in Prentice
Park. Update: National Guard was
playing war games in the park.

Caller reported that while they
were gone this week, someone
moved into their house and
appeared to be living there.

(Not fun anymore ... )
Caller reported a possible
Peeping Tom at her house
for the last month.

Report of a male on top of
a backhoe belonging to C&W
Trucking, beating on it.

Report of a partridge flying in one
window and out the other,
breaking both of them.

## DECEMBER 2004

County jail reported that
a person wandered into the lobby
and asked to go to jail.

Report of assault at a Christmas party on Sanborn Avenue.

Caller reported theft of dirt from his property.

Caller reported that someone rang her doorbell in Washburn.

Report of a woman breaking into a motel and is now sleeping half naked on a bed.

Caller advised that someone drove through her culvert last night ...

Caller reported snowmobiles going off the trail and onto her property and almost hit her snowman.

# 2011

## NOVEMBER 2011

Woman reports a break-in to her residence. Says all she notices missing is some cologne.

# 2012

## FEBRUARY 2012

Caller reports seeing a man enter a bank on Main Street East while leaving his car running.

911 caller in Marengo reports seeing several ducks on the road.

Caller reports a green sedan parked by the gazebo at the marina with the windows fogged up. Caller says people inside seem to be "fooling around."

Caller reports there is a girl sleeping in his driveway.

## MARCH 2012

Caller wants to change her no-contact domestic order so her husband can contact her and fix stuff around the house.

Caller from Washburn reports
a bear in the yard that
is eating their bird feeder.


## APRIL 2012

Caller reports a brown colored
suit has been on the bench by his
window for a few days. Caller says
there is a cell phone and lip gloss
in the suit.


Caller reports a horse and buggy
westbound on 3rd Street West.


Caller wants to know why she has
to pick up her dog droppings when
the people down the road don't
pick up after their horses.


The polling place at the fire station
in Mason reports a pit bull mix is
running loose and chasing voters.

# MAY 2012

Caller reports there is a bear
in their house ...
Caller is outside in the car.

Caller in Eileen reports there is
a horse in his field that is in heat.

Caller on Bayfield Street in
Washburn reports a large bear in
her yard that was spooked away
by a gray wolf. The wolf left but
then another bear came by. Caller
reports all the animals left toward
Memorial Park.

# JUNE 2012

Caller reports someone was in her
house today and she keeps her
house locked up. When she came
home, a tool was missing and the
toilet seat was up.

Call from bus driver stating purse was on the highway and money was floating around in the air.

Caller reports a naked female running down the beach near Lake Shore Drive West and doesn't appear to be in distress.

Caller reports a trapped rabbit. Officer advises it was a cottontail.

Caller requests permission from an officer to sit in the ditch of his parents' house. Caller would like to wait with a shot gun and shoot out the mailbox vandal's radiator on the get-away car when they steal his parent's mailbox.

## JULY 2012

Caller reports someone came onto his property near the corner of State Highways 13 and 77 and cut his clothesline.

Caller reports an ongoing problem
with their neighbor on State
Highway 12, walking around
outside naked.

Report of nude male
in his backyard. Update: Subject
spoken to and said he was outside
with no clothes on because it
was hot. He was advised it would
be best if he would stay inside
high-fenced area of his property.
Subject said he would take care
of the situation.

Caller reports his camper trailer
was stolen over two years ago and
he never reported it but he just
saw it being pulled down the road
on Deer Creek Road.

Caller reports an emu standing
on Whiting Road at Highway 13.

Caller reports there are 16 head
of cattle in the backyard.

Caller reports a 40-year old male who is dancing in the alley since 5:30 this morning behind her residence. Subject has on shorts, flip flops, baseball cap, and a Packer poncho over his head.

## AUGUST 2012

Caller reports her husband left at 8:00 p.m. to go fishing on Lake Namekagon and she has not heard from him since 10:37 p.m. Update: Caller states that although she is not happy with him, he is home and all is well.

Caller reports a young adult outside the grocery part of the store ... who took Crest 3-D Whitening Strips without paying for them. Subject is wearing a brown baseball cap, blue shirt and shorts and is approximately six feet tall and clean shaven. (and has yellow teeth)

Resident reports a male passed
out on her porch swing ...

## SEPTEMBER 2012

Caller thinks there are people in
her attic on Prentice Avenue.

Caller reports a male
"drunker than a fart" last
seen heading west ...

Caller reports hitting a couch that
is in the middle of Highway 13.

Caller reports the theft of a bald
eagle from her freezer ...

## OCTOBER 2012

... caller just woke up and a
horrible thing went through her
head and she would like her
husband evicted.

Caller reports an oven fire with no flames showing, large amount of black smoke coming from inside and believes the back wall behind the oven may be on fire ... Second call from resident reports bottom of her pie fell onto the heating element ...

An officer came upon a vehicle with egg on it.

## DECEMBER 2012

(Probably didn't need markings)
Caller reports theft of Christmas decoration – lighted buck deer that moves ... Caller does have it marked if it is found.

Goodwill reports dumpster diving. She told him he was not allowed to be in the store's dumpster. Male said he did it all the time and was told by his friend that it was okay. Caller advised to call police if anyone else is found in dumpster.

# 2013

## JANUARY 2013

Caller states he needs an ambulance. Nurse online tells him to call for an ambulance.

Caller in Washburn reports his mother owns the Dairy Queen and has received reports of someone building up snow in the back for a snowboard ramp.

## THANK YOU
## DEAR READER

for getting all the way to the end. By now, you will probably be happy to know that there were MANY more "cows in the road" than I included in the book.

— R.N.

CPSIA information can be obtained at www.ICGtesting.com
Printed in the USA
LVOW06s0459211013

357765LV00001B/1/P